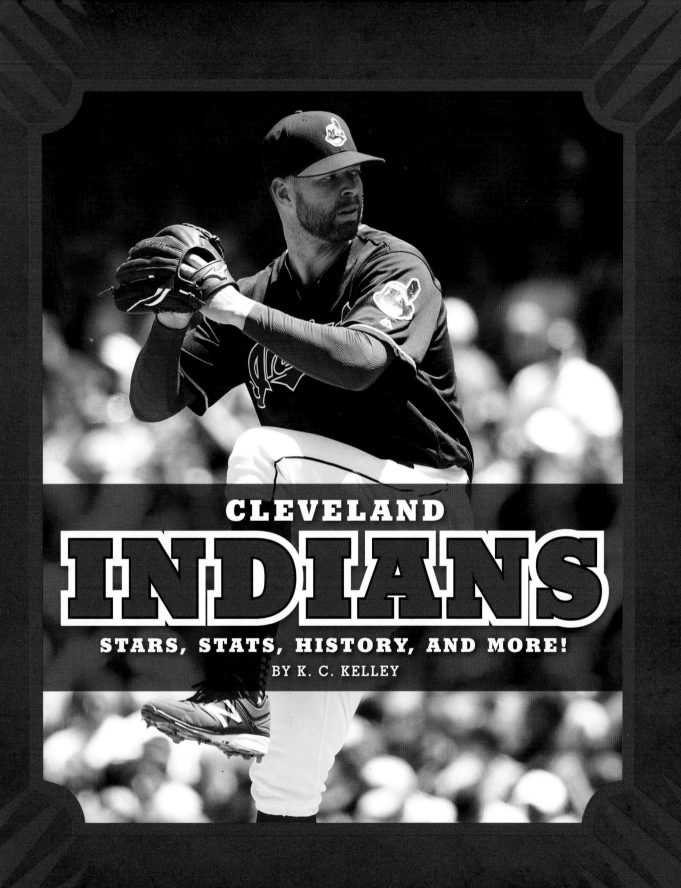

CLEVELAND
INDIANS
STARS, STATS, HISTORY, AND MORE!
BY K. C. KELLEY

childsworld.com

Published by The Child's World®
1980 Lookout Drive • Mankato, MN 56003-1705
800-599-READ • www.childsworld.com

ISBN 9781-503828216
LCCN 2018944834

Printed in the United States of America
PAO2392

Photo Credits:
Cover: Joe Robbins (2).
Interior: AP Images: Cal Sports Media 19, Amy Sancetta
20; Dreamstime.com: Jerry Coli 23; Library of Congress:
8; Newscom: Aaron Josefczyk/UPI 11; Nick Wosicka/Icon
SW 27; Phil Masturzo/KRT 17; Joe Robbins 4, 7, 12,
14, 24, 29.

About the Author

K.C. Kelley is a huge sports
fan who has written more
than 100 books for kids. His
favorite sport is baseball.
He has also written about
football, basketball, soccer,
and even auto racing! He lives
in Santa Barbara, California.

On the Cover

Main photo: Pitcher Corey Kluber
Inset: Hall of Famer Bob Feller

CONTENTS

GO, CLEVELAND!

he Cleveland Indians have been one of baseball's best teams in the past few seasons. They have a great group of top young players. The team's fans love it! They have waited for their team to improve. Will they see a World Series win soon? Let's meet the team some fans call "the **Tribe**"!

◄ *Francisco Lindor is one of baseball's most exciting young players.*

WHO ARE THE INDIANS?

**C**leveland plays in the American League (AL). That group is part of Major League Baseball (MLB). MLB also includes the National League (NL). There are 30 teams in MLB. The winner of the AL plays the winner of the NL in the **World Series**. The Indians haven't won the World Series since 1948. Their fans can't wait for another title!

José Ramirez is a home run threat for Cleveland. ➤

WHERE THEY CAME FROM

Cleveland was one of the first teams in the AL in 1901. The team was called the Blues that year. In 1902, they were the Bronchos. In 1903, the team started calling itself the Naps. That was for manager and star player Napoleon Lajoie. The team became the Indians in 1915.

◄ *Hall of Famer Napoleon Lajoie's name was pronounced LA-zhe-way.*

WHO THEY PLAY

The Indians play in the AL Central Division. The other teams in the AL Central are the Chicago White Sox, the Detroit Tigers, the Kansas City Royals, and the Minnesota Twins. The Indians play more games against their division **rivals** than against other teams. In all, the Indians play 162 games each season. They play 81 games at home and 81 on the road.

Francisco Lindor and Lonnie Chisenhall ➤
high-five after another Cleveland win.

WHERE THEY PLAY

The Indians used to play in a football stadium. Cleveland Stadium was huge and hardly ever filled up for baseball games. In 1994, Jacobs Field opened and changed baseball in Cleveland. The ballpark was a huge hit. It was beautiful and comfortable. Fans poured in to see their heroes. In 2008, a company paid to rename the ballpark Progressive Field.

◄ *By whatever name, the Indians' home is one of baseball's nicest ballparks.*

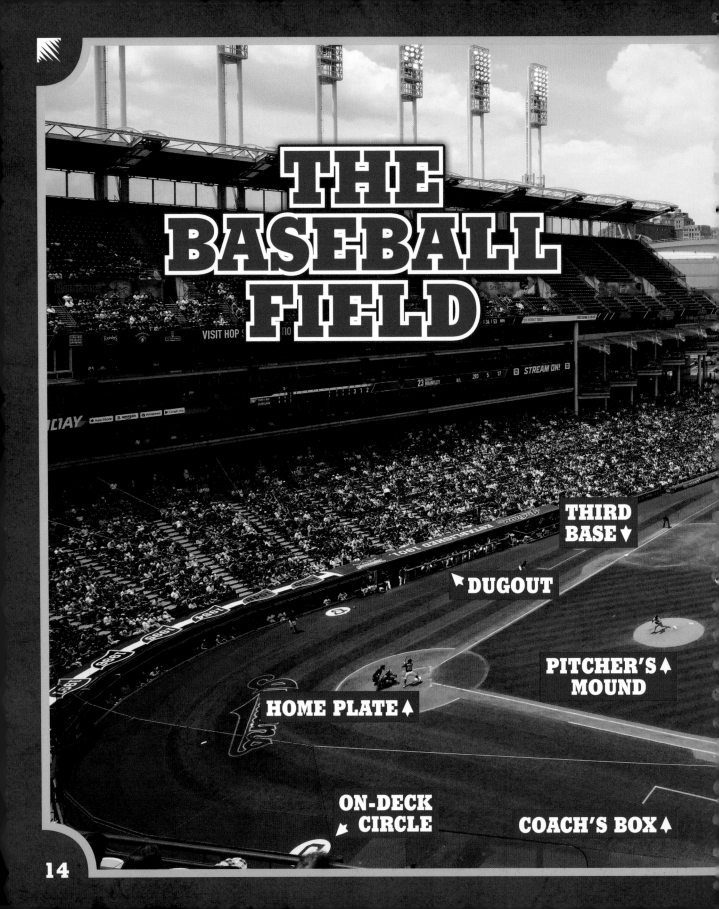

THE BASEBALL FIELD

THIRD BASE ▼

◤ DUGOUT

PITCHER'S ▲
MOUND

HOME PLATE ▲

ON-DECK
▼ CIRCLE

COACH'S BOX ▲

FOUL LINE

OUTFIELD

SECOND BASE

INFIELD

FIRST BASE

FOUL LINE

The Indians have had a lot of great days in their long history. Here are a few of them.

1920—Cleveland won its very first World Series. The Tribe defeated the NL-champion Brooklyn Dodgers.

1954—The Indians won the American League. They set a team record by winning 111 games.

1995—The Indians won their first AL **pennant** since 1954! They lost the World Series to the Atlanta Braves, but it was a great year in Cleveland!

Omar Vizquel and Jim Thome celebrate the ➤
Indians' 1995 AL championship.

TOUGH DAYS

Like every team, the Indians have had some not-so-great days, too. Here are a few their fans might not want to recall.

1908—The Indians missed making it to the World Series by a half-game!

1991—Cleveland had some tough seasons in the early 1990s. They lost 105 games in 1991. That was their most ever.

2016—The Indians came within one game of a World Series title. They lost Game 7 to the Chicago Cubs in 10 innings.

Anthony Rizzo of the Cubs catches the final ➤
out of the 2016 World Series.

MEET THE FANS!

ndians fans have watched a lot of pretty bad teams. They stuck with their hometown heroes, though. In recent years, they have seen some of baseball's best! Some Indians fans bring huge drums to beat during games. This gets the crowd fired up!

◀ *Cleveland fan John Adams has been banging his drum for the team for many years.*

HEROES THEN

leveland has had lots of stars in its long history. Outfielder Earl Averill was a six-time All-Star and a **Hall of Famer**. Bob Feller threw one of baseball's fastest pitches. He could throw more than 100 miles per hour! In 1947, All-Star outfielder Larry Doby became the first African American in the AL. More recently, Jim Thome was a big slugger. He hit 612 homers, most of them for Cleveland. Shortstop Omar Vizquel was one of the best ever at fielding his position.

In 2018, Jim Thome was named to the Baseball Hall of Fame. ➤

HEROES NOW

**T**hird baseman José Ramirez is one of the AL's best hitters. He led the league in **doubles** in 2017. Shortstop Francisco Lindor combines great fielding with super hitting. His big smile also lights up the diamond! Pitcher Corey Kluber is one of baseball's best. He won the 2017 **Cy Young Award** as the top AL pitcher. Carlos Carrasco throws a great fastball for lots of strikeouts.

◄ *Corey Kluber has one of baseball's best curveballs.*

GEARING UP

aseball players wear team uniforms. On defense, they wear leather gloves to catch the ball. As batters, they wear hard helmets. This protects them from pitches. Batters hit the ball with long wood bats. Each player chooses his own size of bat. Catchers have the toughest job. They wear a lot of protection.

THE BASEBALL

The outside of the Major League baseball is made from cow leather. Two leather pieces shaped like 8s are stitched together. There are 108 stitches of red thread. These stitches help players grip the ball. Inside, the ball has a small center of cork and rubber. Hundreds of feet of yarn are tightly wound around this center.

CATCHER'S MASK
AND HELMET

PITCH
CHART

CHEST
PROTECTOR ▸

◂ CATCHER'S
MITT

◂ SHIN GUARDS

CATCHER'S GEAR

TEAM STATS

Here are some of the all-time career records for the Cleveland Indians. All of these stats are through the 2018 regular season.

HOME RUNS	
Jim Thome	337
Albert Belle	242

RBI	
Earl Averill	1,084
Jim Thome	937

BATTING AVERAGE	
Shoeless Joe Jackson	.375
Tris Speaker	.354

STOLEN BASES	
Kenny Lofton	452
Omar Vizquel	279

WINS	
Bob Feller	266
Mel Harder	223

SAVES	
Cody Allen	149
Bob Wickman	139

Bob Feller used an awesome fastball to become an all-time great. ➤

STRIKEOUTS

Bob Feller	2,581
Sam McDowell	2,159

GLOSSARY

Cy Young Award (SIGH YUNG uh-WARD) honor given to the top pitcher in each league

doubles (DUB-uls) hits on which the batter reaches second base

Hall of Famer (HALL UV FAY-mer) a player honored by being included in the Hall of Fame building in Cooperstown, New York

pennant (PEN-ant) a triangle-shaped flag given to the winner of each league

rivals (RYE-vuhlz) two people or groups competing for the same thing

tribe (TRYB) a group of people with similar interests or common ancestors

World Series (WURLD SEE-reez) the annual championship of Major League Baseball

FIND OUT MORE

IN THE LIBRARY

Connery-Boyd, Peg. *Cleveland Indians: Big Book of Activities*. Chicago, IL: Sourcebooks Jabberwocky, 2016.

Crowe, Chris. *Just as Good: How Larry Doby Changed America's Game*. Boston, MA: Candlewick, 2012.

Rhodes, Sam. *Cleveland Indians* (Inside MLB). Calgary, AB: Weigl, 2018.

ON THE WEB

Visit our website for links about the Cleveland Indians:
childsworld.com/links

Note to Parents, Teachers, and Librarians: We routinely verify our web links to make sure they are safe and active sites. So encourage your readers to check them out!

INDEX